My plant Journal

Watering and Care Log

Julie Marr Studios

ASPEN STREET PRESS

Colorado

TABLE OF CONTENTS

Plant Information

Plant Name
Location in House

Light Preference	Growth Rate

Fertilizing Instructions

Repotting Dates

Plant Concerns

Drawing of Plant

WATERING NEEDS

Preferred Water Level   Best Misting Frequency

_____

WATERING DATES

NOTES

_____

_____

_____

ADDITIONAL PLANT NOTES

PLANT INFORMATION

Plant Name
Location in House

Light Preference	Growth Rate

Fertilizing Instructions

Repotting Dates

Plant Concerns

Drawing of Plant

WATERING NEEDS

Preferred Water Level   Best Misting Frequency

_____

WATERING DATES

NOTES

_____

_____

_____

ADDITIONAL PLANT NOTES

Plant Information

Plant Name
Location in House

Light Preference	**Growth Rate**

Fertilizing Instructions

Repotting Dates

Plant Concerns

Drawing of Plant

WATERING NEEDS

Preferred Water Level   Best Misting Frequency

_____

WATERING DATES

NOTES

_____

_____

_____

PLANT INFORMATION

Plant Name
Location in House

Light Preference	Growth Rate

Fertilizing Instructions

Repotting Dates

Plant Concerns

Drawing of Plant

WATERING NEEDS

Preferred Water Level   Best Misting Frequency

_____

WATERING DATES

_____	_____	_____	_____	_____
_____	_____	_____	_____	_____
_____	_____	_____	_____	_____
_____	_____	_____	_____	_____
_____	_____	_____	_____	_____
_____	_____	_____	_____	_____
_____	_____	_____	_____	_____
_____	_____	_____	_____	_____
_____	_____	_____	_____	_____
_____	_____	_____	_____	_____
_____	_____	_____	_____	_____
_____	_____	_____	_____	_____
_____	_____	_____	_____	_____
_____	_____	_____	_____	_____

NOTES

_____

_____

_____

ADDITIONAL PLANT NOTES

PLANT INFORMATION

Plant Name
Location in House

Light Preference	Growth Rate

Fertilizing Instructions

Repotting Dates

Plant Concerns

Drawing of Plant

WATERING NEEDS

Preferred Water Level   Best Misting Frequency

_____

WATERING DATES

NOTES

_____

_____

_____

21

ADDITIONAL PLANT NOTES

Plant Information

Plant Name
Plant Name
Location in House

Light Preference	**Growth Rate**

Fertilizing Instructions

Repotting Dates

Plant Concerns

_____

_____

_____

_____

_____

Drawing of Plant

WATERING NEEDS

Preferred Water Level   Best Misting Frequency

_____

WATERING DATES

NOTES

_____

_____

_____

PLANT INFORMATION

Plant Name

Location in House

Light Preference	Growth Rate

Fertilizing Instructions

Repotting Dates

Plant Concerns

Drawing of Plant

WATERING NEEDS

Preferred Water Level   Best Misting Frequency

_____

WATERING DATES

NOTES

_____

_____

_____

ADDITIONAL PLANT NOTES

Plant Information

Plant Name
Location in House

Light Preference	Growth Rate

Fertilizing Instructions

Repotting Dates

Plant Concerns

Drawing of Plant

WATERING NEEDS

Preferred Water Level   Best Misting Frequency

_____

WATERING DATES

_____ _____ _____ _____ _____

_____ _____ _____ _____ _____

_____ _____ _____ _____ _____

_____ _____ _____ _____ _____

_____ _____ _____ _____ _____

_____ _____ _____ _____ _____

_____ _____ _____ _____ _____

_____ _____ _____ _____ _____

_____ _____ _____ _____ _____

_____ _____ _____ _____ _____

_____ _____ _____ _____ _____

_____ _____ _____ _____ _____

_____ _____ _____ _____ _____

_____ _____ _____ _____ _____

NOTES

_____

_____

_____

PLANT INFORMATION

Plant Name
Location in House

Light Preference	**Growth Rate**

Fertilizing Instructions

Repotting Dates

Plant Concerns

Drawing of Plant

WATERING NEEDS

Preferred Water Level   Best Misting Frequency

_____

WATERING DATES

_____	_____	_____	_____	_____
_____	_____	_____	_____	_____
_____	_____	_____	_____	_____
_____	_____	_____	_____	_____
_____	_____	_____	_____	_____
_____	_____	_____	_____	_____
_____	_____	_____	_____	_____
_____	_____	_____	_____	_____
_____	_____	_____	_____	_____
_____	_____	_____	_____	_____
_____	_____	_____	_____	_____
_____	_____	_____	_____	_____
_____	_____	_____	_____	_____

NOTES

_____

_____

_____

PLANT INFORMATION

Plant Name
Location in House

Light Preference	**Growth Rate**

Fertilizing Instructions

Repotting Dates

Plant Concerns

Drawing of Plant

WATERING NEEDS

Preferred Water Level   Best Misting Frequency

_____

WATERING DATES

_____	_____	_____	_____	_____
_____	_____	_____	_____	_____
_____	_____	_____	_____	_____
_____	_____	_____	_____	_____
_____	_____	_____	_____	_____
_____	_____	_____	_____	_____
_____	_____	_____	_____	_____
_____	_____	_____	_____	_____
_____	_____	_____	_____	_____
_____	_____	_____	_____	_____
_____	_____	_____	_____	_____
_____	_____	_____	_____	_____
_____	_____	_____	_____	_____
_____	_____	_____	_____	_____

NOTES

_____

_____

_____

ADDITIONAL PLANT NOTES

PLANT INFORMATION

Plant Name
Location in House

Light Preference	**Growth Rate**

Fertilizing Instructions

Repotting Dates

Plant Concerns

Drawing of Plant

WATERING NEEDS

Preferred Water Level   Best Misting Frequency

      _____

WATERING DATES

_____ _____ _____ _____ _____

_____ _____ _____ _____ _____

_____ _____ _____ _____ _____

_____ _____ _____ _____ _____

_____ _____ _____ _____ _____

_____ _____ _____ _____ _____

_____ _____ _____ _____ _____

_____ _____ _____ _____ _____

_____ _____ _____ _____ _____

_____ _____ _____ _____ _____

_____ _____ _____ _____ _____

_____ _____ _____ _____ _____

_____ _____ _____ _____ _____

NOTES

_____

_____

_____

ADDITIONAL PLANT NOTES

Plant Information

Plant Name
Location in House

Light Preference	Growth Rate

Fertilizing Instructions

Repotting Dates

Plant Concerns

Drawing of Plant

WATERING NEEDS

Preferred Water Level   Best Misting Frequency

_____

WATERING DATES

NOTES

_____

_____

_____

ADDITIONAL PLANT NOTES

PLANT INFORMATION

Plant Name
Location in House

Light Preference	**Growth Rate**

Fertilizing Instructions

Repotting Dates

Plant Concerns

Drawing of Plant

WATERING NEEDS

Preferred Water Level   Best Misting Frequency

_____

WATERING DATES

_____ _____ _____ _____ _____

_____ _____ _____ _____ _____

_____ _____ _____ _____ _____

_____ _____ _____ _____ _____

_____ _____ _____ _____ _____

_____ _____ _____ _____ _____

_____ _____ _____ _____ _____

_____ _____ _____ _____ _____

_____ _____ _____ _____ _____

_____ _____ _____ _____ _____

_____ _____ _____ _____ _____

_____ _____ _____ _____ _____

_____ _____ _____ _____ _____

NOTES

_____

_____

_____

ADDITIONAL PLANT NOTES

PLANT INFORMATION

Plant Name
Location in House

Light Preference	Growth Rate

Fertilizing Instructions

Repotting Dates

Plant Concerns

Drawing of Plant

WATERING NEEDS

Preferred Water Level   Best Misting Frequency

_____

WATERING DATES

___	___	___	___	___
___	___	___	___	___
___	___	___	___	___
___	___	___	___	___
___	___	___	___	___
___	___	___	___	___
___	___	___	___	___
___	___	___	___	___
___	___	___	___	___
___	___	___	___	___
___	___	___	___	___
___	___	___	___	___
___	___	___	___	___
___	___	___	___	___

NOTES

_____

_____

_____

ADDITIONAL PLANT NOTES

PLANT INFORMATION

Plant Name

Location in House

Light Preference	Growth Rate

Fertilizing Instructions

Repotting Dates

Plant Concerns

Drawing of Plant

WATERING NEEDS

Preferred Water Level

Best Misting Frequency

_____

WATERING DATES

NOTES

_____

_____

_____

ADDITIONAL PLANT NOTES

PLANT INFORMATION

Plant Name
Location in House

Light Preference	Growth Rate

Fertilizing Instructions

Repotting Dates

Plant Concerns

Drawing of Plant

WATERING NEEDS

Preferred Water Level   Best Misting Frequency

_____

WATERING DATES

_____ _____ _____ _____ _____

_____ _____ _____ _____ _____

_____ _____ _____ _____ _____

_____ _____ _____ _____ _____

_____ _____ _____ _____ _____

_____ _____ _____ _____ _____

_____ _____ _____ _____ _____

_____ _____ _____ _____ _____

_____ _____ _____ _____ _____

_____ _____ _____ _____ _____

_____ _____ _____ _____ _____

_____ _____ _____ _____ _____

_____ _____ _____ _____ _____

_____ _____ _____ _____ _____

NOTES

_____

_____

_____

ADDITIONAL PLANT NOTES

PLANT INFORMATION

Plant Name

Location in House

Light Preference	Growth Rate

Fertilizing Instructions

Repotting Dates

Plant Concerns

Drawing of Plant

WATERING NEEDS

Preferred Water Level   Best Misting Frequency

   _____

WATERING DATES

_____ _____ _____ _____ _____

_____ _____ _____ _____ _____

_____ _____ _____ _____ _____

_____ _____ _____ _____ _____

_____ _____ _____ _____ _____

_____ _____ _____ _____ _____

_____ _____ _____ _____ _____

_____ _____ _____ _____ _____

_____ _____ _____ _____ _____

_____ _____ _____ _____ _____

_____ _____ _____ _____ _____

_____ _____ _____ _____ _____

_____ _____ _____ _____ _____

NOTES

_____

_____

_____

PLANT INFORMATION

Plant Name
Location in House

Light Preference	Growth Rate

Fertilizing Instructions

Repotting Dates

Plant Concerns

Drawing of Plant

WATERING NEEDS

Preferred Water Level   Best Misting Frequency

_____

WATERING DATES

NOTES

_____

_____

_____

ADDITIONAL PLANT NOTES

PLANT INFORMATION

Plant Name
Location in House

Light Preference	**Growth Rate**

Fertilizing Instructions

Repotting Dates

Plant Concerns

Drawing of Plant

WATERING NEEDS

Preferred Water Level   Best Misting Frequency

_____

WATERING DATES

_____ _____ _____ _____ _____

_____ _____ _____ _____ _____

_____ _____ _____ _____ _____

_____ _____ _____ _____ _____

_____ _____ _____ _____ _____

_____ _____ _____ _____ _____

_____ _____ _____ _____ _____

_____ _____ _____ _____ _____

_____ _____ _____ _____ _____

_____ _____ _____ _____ _____

_____ _____ _____ _____ _____

_____ _____ _____ _____ _____

_____ _____ _____ _____ _____

_____ _____ _____ _____ _____

NOTES

_____

_____

_____

ADDITIONAL PLANT NOTES

PLANT INFORMATION

Plant Name	
Location in House	
Light Preference	**Growth Rate**
Fertilizing Instructions	

Repotting Dates

Plant Concerns

Drawing of Plant

WATERING NEEDS

Preferred Water Level   Best Misting Frequency

   _____

WATERING DATES

NOTES

_____

_____

_____

PLANT INFORMATION

Plant Name
Location in House

Light Preference	Growth Rate

Fertilizing Instructions

Repotting Dates

Plant Concerns

Drawing of Plant

WATERING NEEDS

Preferred Water Level   Best Misting Frequency

_____

WATERING DATES

NOTES

_____

_____

_____

PLANT INFORMATION

Plant Name
Location in House

Light Preference	**Growth Rate**

Fertilizing Instructions

Repotting Dates

Plant Concerns

_____

_____

_____

_____

_____

Drawing of Plant

WATERING NEEDS

Preferred Water Level   Best Misting Frequency

   _____

WATERING DATES

_____ _____ _____ _____ _____

_____ _____ _____ _____ _____

_____ _____ _____ _____ _____

_____ _____ _____ _____ _____

_____ _____ _____ _____ _____

_____ _____ _____ _____ _____

_____ _____ _____ _____ _____

_____ _____ _____ _____ _____

_____ _____ _____ _____ _____

_____ _____ _____ _____ _____

_____ _____ _____ _____ _____

_____ _____ _____ _____ _____

_____ _____ _____ _____ _____

NOTES

_____

_____

_____

ADDITIONAL PLANT NOTES

PLANT INFORMATION

Plant Name
Location in House

Light Preference	**Growth Rate**

Fertilizing Instructions

Repotting Dates

Plant Concerns

Drawing of Plant

WATERING NEEDS

Preferred Water Level   Best Misting Frequency

_____

WATERING DATES

_____ _____ _____ _____ _____

_____ _____ _____ _____ _____

_____ _____ _____ _____ _____

_____ _____ _____ _____ _____

_____ _____ _____ _____ _____

_____ _____ _____ _____ _____

_____ _____ _____ _____ _____

_____ _____ _____ _____ _____

_____ _____ _____ _____ _____

_____ _____ _____ _____ _____

_____ _____ _____ _____ _____

_____ _____ _____ _____ _____

_____ _____ _____ _____ _____

_____ _____ _____ _____ _____

_____ _____ _____ _____ _____

_____ _____ _____ _____ _____

NOTES

_____

_____

_____

ADDITIONAL PLANT NOTES

PLANT INFORMATION

Plant Name	
Location in House	

Light Preference	**Growth Rate**

Fertilizing Instructions

Repotting Dates

Plant Concerns

Drawing of Plant

WATERING NEEDS

Preferred Water Level   Best Misting Frequency

_____

WATERING DATES

NOTES

_____

_____

_____

PLANT INFORMATION

Plant Name

Location in House

Light Preference	Growth Rate

Fertilizing Instructions

Repotting Dates

Plant Concerns

Drawing of Plant

WATERING NEEDS

Preferred Water Level   Best Misting Frequency

_____

WATERING DATES

_____ _____ _____ _____ _____

_____ _____ _____ _____ _____

_____ _____ _____ _____ _____

_____ _____ _____ _____ _____

_____ _____ _____ _____ _____

_____ _____ _____ _____ _____

_____ _____ _____ _____ _____

_____ _____ _____ _____ _____

_____ _____ _____ _____ _____

_____ _____ _____ _____ _____

_____ _____ _____ _____ _____

_____ _____ _____ _____ _____

_____ _____ _____ _____ _____

NOTES

_____

_____

_____

ADDITIONAL PLANT NOTES

PLANT INFORMATION

Plant Name	
Location in House	
Light Preference	**Growth Rate**
Fertilizing Instructions	

Repotting Dates

Plant Concerns

Drawing of Plant

WATERING NEEDS

Preferred Water Level   Best Misting Frequency

     _____

WATERING DATES

_____ _____ _____ _____ _____

_____ _____ _____ _____ _____

_____ _____ _____ _____ _____

_____ _____ _____ _____ _____

_____ _____ _____ _____ _____

_____ _____ _____ _____ _____

_____ _____ _____ _____ _____

_____ _____ _____ _____ _____

_____ _____ _____ _____ _____

_____ _____ _____ _____ _____

_____ _____ _____ _____ _____

_____ _____ _____ _____ _____

_____ _____ _____ _____ _____

_____ _____ _____ _____ _____

NOTES

_____

_____

_____

ADDITIONAL PLANT NOTES

PLANT INFORMATION

Plant Name
Location in House

Light Preference	**Growth Rate**

Fertilizing Instructions

Repotting Dates

Plant Concerns

Drawing of Plant

WATERING NEEDS

Preferred Water Level   Best Misting Frequency

_____

WATERING DATES

NOTES

_____

_____

_____

ADDITIONAL PLANT NOTES

PLANT INFORMATION

Plant Name
Location in House

Light Preference	Growth Rate

Fertilizing Instructions

Repotting Dates

Plant Concerns

Drawing of Plant

WATERING NEEDS

Preferred Water Level   Best Misting Frequency

   _____

WATERING DATES

_____	_____	_____	_____	_____
_____	_____	_____	_____	_____
_____	_____	_____	_____	_____
_____	_____	_____	_____	_____
_____	_____	_____	_____	_____
_____	_____	_____	_____	_____
_____	_____	_____	_____	_____
_____	_____	_____	_____	_____
_____	_____	_____	_____	_____
_____	_____	_____	_____	_____
_____	_____	_____	_____	_____
_____	_____	_____	_____	_____
_____	_____	_____	_____	_____

NOTES

_____

_____

_____

PLANT INFORMATION

Plant Name

Location in House

Light Preference	Growth Rate

Fertilizing Instructions

Repotting Dates

Plant Concerns

Drawing of Plant

WATERING NEEDS

Preferred Water Level   Best Misting Frequency

_____

WATERING DATES

_____ _____ _____ _____ _____
_____ _____ _____ _____ _____
_____ _____ _____ _____ _____
_____ _____ _____ _____ _____
_____ _____ _____ _____ _____
_____ _____ _____ _____ _____
_____ _____ _____ _____ _____
_____ _____ _____ _____ _____
_____ _____ _____ _____ _____
_____ _____ _____ _____ _____
_____ _____ _____ _____ _____
_____ _____ _____ _____ _____
_____ _____ _____ _____ _____

NOTES

_____

_____

_____

ADDITIONAL PLANT NOTES

PLANT INFORMATION

Plant Name
Location in House

Light Preference	**Growth Rate**

Fertilizing Instructions

Repotting Dates

Plant Concerns

Drawing of Plant

WATERING NEEDS

Preferred Water Level   Best Misting Frequency

_____

WATERING DATES

NOTES

_____

_____

_____

ADDITIONAL PLANT NOTES

Printed in Great Britain
by Amazon

65767780R00078